HOW TO

CREATE

BEST SELLING BRAND ON

ANY **MARKETPLACE**

JAMES BRIAN

©2019 ALL RIGHTS RESERVED

No part of this publication may be reproduced or transmitted in any means. Mechanical or electronic, including photocopying and recording, or by any information storage and retrieval system, without permission in writing from author or publisher (except by a review, who may quote brief passage and/or show brief video clips in a review)

CONTACT: shomatth@gmail.com

CONTENT

INTRODUCTION

BRANDING

HOW TO DEVELOP A BRAND

CHOOSING A BRAND NAME

PICKING THE RIGHT FONT AND COLOR

CREATING A PERFECT LOGO

SOME LOGO CONCEPT

BRAND SLOGAN

CHARACTERISTICS OF SUCCESSFUL BRANDS

INTRODUCTION

Are you planning selling a product? Or you already own a product and don't know how to go about it, I have good news for you. The way out is branding, this is the power house of establishing yourself and your product to the outside world. Have you ever imagined how Amazon, Alibaba and others make their names? They all enforced the power of branding.

The business world is not for only expert rather for those ready to follow and work according to the rules guiding it. The business tycoon of today started as a novice, if they succeed why won't you? As a new seller in the market buyer needs to recognize your product. The only and best way is branding.

THIS BOOK is well written to provide you with amazing, unique and easy way to launch your product into the business world with a guarantee of success.

BRANDING

A brand is a unique name, design, symbol, or other feature that distinguishes an organization or product from other product in the eyes and mind of the customer. It's used in business, for marketing, and advertisement.

Branding is very important for businesses whether big or small, many corporate brands try to look more like small firms in order to appeal to consumers that prefer to support independent brands. There is need to recognize the link between successful businesses and strong branding and aspire to develop a brand that creates similar success for themselves.

BRANDING IS NOT

A brand isn't just a recognizable logo and name that distinguishes you in a crowded market or how your business is perceived externally. only few sellers realize that successful brands have this branding at the heart of the business. So much that in many ways that it almost substitutes the word brand for business.

BRANDING IS

Branding is a way of defining your business to yourself, your team and your external audiences. It could be called the business' 'identity', but only on the understanding that it embodies the core of what the business is and its values, not just what it looks and sounds like. Brand building is deliberate and skillful application of effort to create a desired perception in someone else's mind. Developing the best brand encourages loyalty, advocacy. It can even help your price in times when competitors rely on promotional discounts to drive sales. Your brand also gives you the ideal platform from which to extend your product.

HOW TO DEVELOP A BRAND

You can't develop a brand without being consistent and maintaining that consistency as you extend your brand to every part of your business. But it all starts with establishing what that consistency is going to look like and the feeling you want it to evoke. Here I will provide in details of what you need to consider to achieve success for your products.

The following will help you to develop best-selling brand:

1. What's your place in the Market

For you to have a product, you must have carried out research to know who your buyer is and where they are. With this you have set your business on the right place. If you have not, no need to panic, I will tell you how to go about it. One need to be at the top of the game, because there are lot of competitor out there.

There are many ways to do this:

- ✓ Google your product or service category to know who your competitor is then formulate means on how to be ahead of them.

- ✓ Check subreddits that relate to your customers and eavesdrop on their conversations and product recommendations.
- ✓ Relate with people who are part of your target market and ask them what brands they prefer to buy in your space.
- ✓ Look at the relevant social media accounts or pages your target audience follows and are receptive to.
- ✓ Go shopping online and offline, get a feel for how your customers would browse and buy products which they want.

As you go about your research, make a note of:

1. Who your customers are, the ones you can easily sell to.
2. Who your top competitors are, the brands that are established and known in the market.
3. How your customers speak and what they talk about—the interests they have and the language they express them in.

It's important to have a handle on this before moving forward as it will inform what your brand should focus on and how it can position itself apart from competitors.

❖ Define Your Brand's Focus and Personality

Your brand can't be everything to everyone, especially at the start. It's important to find your focus and let that inform all the other parts of your brand as you build it.

Here are some questions and branding exercises to get you thinking about the focus and tone of your brand.

What's your positioning statement?

A positioning statement is one or two lines that stake your claim in the market. This isn't necessarily something you put on your website or business card—it's just to help you answer the right questions about your brand.

e.g. We offer water bottles for hikers to stay hydrated while reducing their carbon footprint. Unlike other water bottle brands, we plant a tree for every bottle you buy.

Your unique selling proposition is the one thing you're competing on. Find it, go in on it, and make it a part of your brand's messaging.

Alternatively, if the company you want to start has a cause at its core (e.g. if you're starting a social enterprise), you can also write this out as a mission statement that makes a clear promise to your customers or to the world.

What words would you associate with your brand?

One way to look at your brand is as if it was a person. What would he or she be like? What kind personality would your customers be attracted to?

This will help inform your voice on social media and the tone of all your creative, both visual and written.

A fun and useful branding exercise is to pitch 3-5 adjectives that describe the type of brand that might resonate with your audience. I compiled this list of traits to help you get started.

What metaphors or concepts describe your brand?

Thinking about your brand as a metaphor or personifying it can help you identify the individual qualities you want it to have.

This can be a vehicle, an animal, a celebrity, a sports team, anything—as long as it has a prominent reputation in your mind that summons the sort of vibe you want your brand to give off.

For example, if I wanted to create a brand targeting entrepreneurs I might choose to use the raccoon as a starting point: They're scrappy survivors that will do anything to thrive. If your brand was an animal, what animal would it by and why is it like that animal to you?

- ❖ **Apply, Extend and Evolve Your Brand as You Grow**

Building a brand doesn't stop with creating a logo or slogan. You brand needs to exist and remain consistent wherever your customers interact with you, from the theme you choose for your website to the marketing you do to customer service to the way you package and ship your products.

You'll continue to shape and evolve your brand as you expose more customers to it and learn more about who they are are and how to speak to them.

It's important to appreciate that you will never have 100% control over how people perceive your brand.

You can tug customers in the right direction, make a great first impression, and manage your reputation, but you can't control the individual perceptions that exists in each person's mind (say, if they had a bad customer service experience).

All you can do is put your best foot forward at every turn and try to resonate with your core audience. But hopefully at this point, you have the tools, knowledge, and resources to start.

CHOOSING A BRAND NAME

The most important and challenging steps of starting a business is choosing a brand name. Using a right name can make your business or company the talk of the town on the other hands wrong name can lead to failure. When brainstorming a brand name, it should convey the expertise that is Simple, Memorable, Emotional, Distinctive & Positive and uniqueness of the product or service you have developed.

As I've said before, a brand is more than a name. The personality, and reputation of your brand name is what give the name meaning in the market.

Your brand name is the first big commitments you must make, it will impact your logo, your domain, your marketing, and trademark registration.

Ideally, you want a brand name that's hard to imitate and even harder to compete with existing players in the market. If you have plan to expand the product you offer down, consider keeping your brand name broad so that it's easier to pivot than when you chose a brand name based on your product name.

There are rules or guidelines for creating a brand name for your business, these rules help you to make the right decision, you are sure to choose the right name if you follow these simple tips

Target

Probably you're disturb having different ideas in your head. The best way to start the process of choosing a brand name is by reviewing the purpose of your business, considering your mission statement, plan, your unique selling proposition and your target audience. The following questions will guide you as you choose a brand name for your business:

- ✓ What are your biggest priorities for your business name? Do you want it to be easy to pronounce, different and unique, directly related to your products and services, etc.?
- ✓ What do you want people to think and feel when they see your business name?
- ✓ What is your business structure and will your business name use a related abbreviation, such as Inc. or LLC?
- ✓ What are the names of your competition? What do you like and dislike about those business names?
- ✓ Does the length of the name matter? If so, do you want a short name or a longer name?

Brainstorming

After you have outlined the guidelines for choosing your brand name then you need to introduce some creativity in landing your amazing brand name. During brainstorming, ensure you keep your guidelines in mind. If you are finding it hand to arrive at a name, try using name combination or generator.

The following are samples from generated brand names:

- ✓ Reframe an unrelated word like Apple for computers.
- ✓ Use a suggestive word like Buffer.
- ✓ Describe it literally like The Shoe Company
- ✓ Alter a word by removing letters, adding letters or using latin endings like Tumblr (Tumbler).
- ✓ Use the initials of a longer name like HBO (Home Box Office)
- ✓ Combine two words: Pinterest (pin interest) or Facebook (Face + Book)
- ✓ Turn a string of words into an acronym: BMW (Bayerische Motoren Werke)

Knowing fully well that your brand name will determine the domain/URL of your website.

There are also professionals that can visualize and brainstorm a right brand name for you, these professionals are on platform like Upwork, Fiverr and Freelancer.

Availability

Before you officially decide on yours propose brand name, you need to check for its availability to make sure it's not in use. This can best be checked through Google and trademark office.

Register

Once you confirm it uniqueness, you can go ahead and register it.

PICKING THE RIGHT FONT AND COLOR

Apart from designing a logo, brand color and font are also important once you've gotten a name. you'll need to think about how you'll visually represent your brand, namely your colors and typography. This will come in handy when you start to build your website.

Choosing Your Brand Color

Colors don't just define the look of your brand; they also convey the feeling you want to communicate and help you make it consistent across your entire brand. You'll want to choose colors that differentiate you from direct competitors to avoid confusing consumers.

Color psychology isn't an exact science, but it does help to inform the choices you make, especially when it comes to the color you choose for your logo.

This infographic offers a nice overview of the emotions and associations that different colors generally evoke.

Etsy	KICKSTARTER
delight labs	Cadbury

Choosing Your Brand Font

Pick two fonts at most to avoid unnecessarily confusing visitors: one for headings and one for body text (this doesn't include the font you might use in your logo).

You can use Microsoft word software to pick your preferred Font.

Helvetica

Baskerville

CREATING A PERFECT LOGO

A logo is probably one of the first things that come to mind when you think about building a brand. And for good reason. It's the face of your company after all, and could potentially be everywhere that your brand exists.

Ideally, you'll want a logo that's unique, identifiable, and that's scalable to work at all sizes.

Consider all the places where your brand's logo needs to exist, from your website to your Facebook Page's profile picture to even the little "favicons" you see in your current browser tab.

If you have a text logo as your Instagram avatar, for example, it'll be almost impossible to read. To make your life easier, get a square version of your logo that has an icon element that remains recognizable even at smaller sizes.

Notice how the Walmart logo has both the "sparks" icon and the wordmark, which can be used separately.

SOME LOGO CONCEPT

The following are some logo concept you can choose to help you communicate with designers and find a style that makes sense for your brand. Keep the colors and fonts you chose in mind to make sure they work together with your logo to convey your brand.

Abstract:

An abstract logo has no explicit meaning. It's just a shape and colors that you can't easily tie back to anything in the real world.

The benefit of an abstract logo is that it has no innate meaning—you can make this up yourself and bring it to life in your customers' minds.

Mascot:

Mascot logos are often represented by the face of a character. They may humanize your brand, but be aware that they are an antiquated style now and only recommended in certain contexts (e.g. you're deliberately going for a retro look).

Emblem:

Emblem logos are often circular and combine text with an emblem for a bold and regal look. If the design is too complicated, however, they can lose their impact when you shrink them down. But done right, they can make for a memorable style of logo.

Lettermark:

Lettermark logos turn the initials of your full business name into a logo. If you chose a business name with 3 or more words, this might be a style you'd want to consider, especially if the initialism is catchy.

Icon:

An icon logo is your brand represented as a visual metaphor. Unlike an abstract logo, an icon logo suggests something about the product (Twitter's bird is suggestive of the frequent short "tweets" on the platform).

As an unestablished brand, you should stay away from using an icon logo by itself. However, if you're not sure about the kind of logo you want, pairing an icon logo with a wordmark is usually a safe bet.

Wordmark:

Wordmark logos turn your brand name, colors, and font into a visual identity. The problem with wordmarks is that they're often hard to create in a scalable square design and easily lose their legibility when shrunk.

However, you can fix this problem by simply getting an accompanying icon logo or turning the first letter of the wordmark into a separate-but-connected logo, like what Facebook does with the F.

Combination:

Because of the limitations that exist for each logo type, many logos are a combination of styles.

As a new business, and you don't need to choose an icon over a wordmark when you can get the best of both. This make it easier to satisfy the condition of creating a scalable logo while still putting your brand name front and center. McDonalds, for example, can use their iconic golden arches wherever the full wordmark doesn't fit.

Unless you've got design chops of your own, you'll probably be delegating the creation of your logo. You can outsource it for a low cost on Fiverr or run a logo contest on 99Designs.

BRAND SLOGAN

A catchy slogan is a nice-to-have asset—something brief and descriptive that you can put in your Twitter bio, website headline, business card, and anywhere else where you've got very few words to make a big impact.

Keep in mind that you can always change your slogan as you find new angles for marketing. Some brand has changed their slogan many times. For example, Pepsi has used over 30 slogans in the past few decades.

A good slogan is short, catchy, and makes a strong impression. Here are some ways to approach writing a slogan of your own:

- Stake your claim: Death Wish Coffee—"The World's Strongest Coffee"
- Make it a Metaphor: Redbull—"Redbull gives you wings."
- Adopt your customers' attitude: Nike—"Just do it."

- Leverage labels: Cards Against Humanity—"A party game for horrible people".
- Write a rhyme: Folgers Coffee: "The best part of wakin' up is Folgers in your cup."
- Describe it literally: Aritzia—"Women's fashion boutique"

This service is also available on freelancing platform like Fiverr and Upwork, look for seller with high positive numbers of reviews.

CHARACTERISTICS OF SUCCESSFUL BRANDS

Considering the competition that businesses face nowadays, it's more important for seller to stand out and develop a unique identity and value proposition through strategic branding. Effective branding is often at the heart of the companies that thrive. The following are the characteristics of a successful branding for your product.

Passion

While it's certainly possible to build a brand in the short-term without passion, it's almost impossible to sustain it in the long run. When you examine massively successful people like Steve Jobs, they all have a serious passion that keeps propelling them to work hard and continually deliver greatness. That passion leads to enthusiasm and genuine joy, which is infectious.

Consumers often become just as enthusiastic about a product or service, leading to word of mouth advertising and referrals.

Passion also helps businesses persevere through inevitable setbacks.

Audience Knowledge

The best brands have a thorough understanding of the demographics of their target market, what their interests are, and how they communicate. Unless it's a mega chain like Wal-Mart, most businesses have a specific target audience they're pursuing. Understanding the target market is critical because it provides direction for the tone and reach of a marketing campaign, along with the overall identity of a brand, while helping to create an organic, human connection between a business and its audience.

Trying to appeal to everyone can be counterproductive, causing a company's brand to become diluted. Finding the right branding approach requires first understanding the target market.

Uniqueness

Establishing a brand identity requires something distinctive. For instance, Apple has become known worldwide for their innovative products and minimalistic, aesthetic appeal. When it comes to service companies, Domino's Pizza used to guarantee that their pizza would arrive in 30 minutes or it'd be free. In terms of a selling point, TOMS shoes donates a free pair of shoes to a child in need for every pair of shoes that are bought. Creating an identity within a niche doesn't demand a revolutionary idea. It simply needs to have one special thing that separates it from the competition. In reality, it's possible to be "a one trick pony" as long as that trick is really good. Once a company figures out what that is, it can concentrate on it and should gain recognition in time.

Consistency

When consumers come back to a business for repeat sales, they usually expect to receive the same level of quality as they did the first time. Restaurants and their food and service quality are a great example of this.

No one wants to deal with a company they can't rely on for consistency. With so many industries being saturated with competitors, inconsistency is often enough of a reason for consumers to take their business elsewhere.

That's why it's so important to adhere to a certain quality standard with a product or service. An example of a brand who offers amazing consistency is McDonald's. This powerhouse of the fast food world provides patrons with a menu that's consistent across the world. Whether someone orders in Florida or China, they know that a Big Mac is going to taste the same.

Competitiveness

Gaining an edge in today's business world isn't easy. For a brand to make a name for itself, team members should thrive on competition and constantly strive to improve. This is the main principle behind Seahawks Coach Pete Carroll's book, Win Forever, as well as the way he runs the team.

When it comes to the major players in any industry, none simply sit back and hope that their consumers will do the work for them. Instead, they tend to be the movers and shakers who work tirelessly toward building and optimizing their brand, going above and beyond consumer expectations. The end result tends to be a brand that is continually on the cutting edge of its industry.

Exposure

Another big part of being recognized as a distinctive, successful brand is the ability to reach consumers through multiple channels. Obviously, larger companies have an advantage gaining exposure because they usually have a bigger marketing budget and more existing connections. They can pay for television commercials, be featured in globally-recognized magazines, and rank highly in search engine results pages.

However, the Internet and social media have narrowed the gap between small companies and large ones. There are more tools than ever before which offer any company a chance at establishing their brand. By developing a presence on networks like Facebook, Twitter, LinkedIn and Google+, anyone is able to reach almost any consumer.

Leadership

Just like any thriving community or sports team, there's typically an influential leader behind every successful brand. For large companies, this may be the CEO. For smaller ones, it's usually the owner.

To coordinate the efforts of team members and guide a strategic vision for a brand, someone has to step up and steer the ship. The leader resolves complications and acts as a liaison between different departments to keep everyone on the same page. They are also expert motivators and know how to maximize the strengths of different team members.

Reference

Ten ways to build a brand for your small business

https://www.marketingdonut.co.uk/marketing-strategy/branding/ten-ways-to-build-a-brand-for-your-small-business

The Top 7 Characteristics Of Successful Brands

https://www.forbes.com/sites/jaysondemers/2013/11/12/the-top-7-characteristics-of-successful-brands/#26dee1d642f9

How to Start Your Own Brand From Scratch in 7 Steps

https://www.shopify.com.ng/blog/how-to-build-a-brand

5 Tips for Choosing a Great Small Business Name

https://www.thebalancesmb.com/choosing-a-great-small-business-name-2951803

www.ingramcontent.com/pod-product-compliance
Lightning Source LLC
Chambersburg PA
CBHW030549220526
45463CB00007B/3035